THE CARNIVORE COOKBOOK

BY TOM WILSON, MD

All Rights Reserved | Copyright 2020

CONTENTS

INTRODUCTION 7

BASIC RECIPES AND SIDES 14
- Beef Broth 14
- Tallow and Cracklings 16
- Carnivore "Bread" 17
- Livers in a Blanket 18
- Crispy Skin Chips 19
- Beef Pâté 20
- Liver Chips 22
- Salmon Skin Chips 23
- Wrapped Hearts 25
- Shrimp Stuffing 26
- Carn "Bread" Stuffing 28
- Carni Protein Bar 30

BREAKFAST 31
- Carnaffles 31
- Eggs and Bacon Breakfast Meat Sandwich 33
- Carni Muffins 35
- Carncakes 36
- Fish muffins 38
- Lamb Scotch Eggs 40
- Meatballs Surprise 41
- Offal Pie 42
- Bacon Cups 44
- Eggs in a Basket 45

LUNCH & DINNER 47
- Cheesy Wings 47
- Grilled Shrimp 49
- Lengua Carnitas 50
- Sea Bass in Paper 51
- Oxtail Stew 52

- Patsa 53
- Turkish Kokoreç 55
- Greek Magiritsa 57
- Pork Belly Fry 59
- Goat Stew 60
- Pork Pockets with Cheese and Bacon 62
- Spit-Roast Lamb 64
- Butter Quail 66
- Full Carnivore Turducken Masterpiece 67
- Ultimate Beef Burgers 69
- Buttered Scallops 70
- Rabbit Roast 71
- Pluck Kabobs 72

Introduction

That you've picked up this book already shows that none of the diets and health kicks are working for you. You've tried everything – from eating nothing but cabbage soup to intermittent fasting to contemplating veganism, but you still feel lethargic, tired, and concerned about your fitness.

There's no need to despair. There's something you haven't tried yet, and it will change everything about your life up until this point. It's revolutionary, exciting, and challenging to everything the world thinks it knows about how to eat. It's called the carnivore diet, and it brings us back to our roots in the best way.

Unlike these, the carnivore diet isn't *new*. In fact, it's old – older than time itself, some would say! From the moment man emerged from the caves and began to eat meat, this is the way our bodies were primed to feast—no vegetables, no alcohol, no fancy seasonings – just meat, water, and animal products. Sound tough? Surprisingly, it isn't nearly as difficult as you think!

Also known as the ASF (animal-sourced food) or zero-carb diet, the carnivore diet is essentially the direct opposite of the veganism trend. It ignores the fads and gets to the facts: our bodies need protein to flourish. The most extreme carnivores eat nothing but meat, salt, and water. Still, our recipes expand a little to include fish and other animal products like eggs and low-lactose, high-fat dairy products like milk, hard cheese, butter, and bone marrow.

So, what are the health benefits? Well, testimonials claim that there are several. Proponents of the carnivore diet have argued it has made them healthier and fitter. It has helped avoid diabetes and other chronic health conditions and even helps with visual and other sensory problems. It's a step-up from paleo or keto diets for those who want to take that extra step towards their full health and wellbeing potential. There are numerous other benefits, too, and the excitement of each testimonial only emphasizes the bonuses the carnivore diet has to offer.

It's normal to worry about a loss of vitamins or minerals under this diet, but you shouldn't. Our ancestors have been eating animals from time immemorial. They survived just fine without modern nutritionists telling them to eat five fruit and vegetables a day! Why should we be any different? Why would we want to be? Humans have survived this long with what we have. Wouldn't it just be arrogant to consider ourselves better than those who came before us?

Here's a quick rundown of what is and isn't permitted on the diet we're using in this book, which is considered <u>tier 2 – tier 3</u> in the carnivore diet. You can adjust all of these recipes to your own tastes, but we think this is a pretty solid grounding, especially for new meat-eaters!

Good:

- ✓ **Grass-fed beef** – this is your primary meat; the fattier, the better. This includes any kind of fatty steak!
- ✓ **Other meats** (not processed)
- ✓ **Roasts** like brisket or ribs
- ✓ **Ground meat**, again, especially beef.
- ✓ **Offal (organ meats)** – this includes sweetbreads (pancreas and thymus gland), liver, kidneys, tongue, heart, brain, and tripe (animal stomach lining)
- ✓ **Poultry (domestic fowl)** – the birds grown for food and eggs, like chickens, geese, turkeys, ducks, pigeons, and guinea fowl.
- ✓ **Fish** – Protein and Omega-3 are essential, and they can be found in fish like salmon, cod, herring, trout, bass, mackerel, sardines, tuna, and more.
- ✓ **Shellfish** – Oysters, scallops, shrimp, mussels, squid, and more.
- ✓ **Eggs** – including duck eggs, chicken eggs, goose eggs, and more
- ✓ **Bone marrow** (red or yellow)
- ✓ **Butter**
- ✓ **Lard and tallow** (animal fats)
- ✓ **Pepper**
- ✓ **Salt**
- ✓ **Bone broth (broth made from boiled bones as stock)**
- ✓ **Water**

Acceptable (depending on strictness level):

- **Cheese** (preferably hard cheeses like Cheddar, Parmigiano, Gruyere, and Pecorino).
- **Yogurt** (high fat low lactose)
- **Milk** (again, high fat, low lactose, from cows, goats, sheep, etc.)
- Some people also continue to drink **teas and coffees**, though they are plant-based, so others do not.
- **Honey**- this depends entirely on what works for your body. Some think it is fine, and some think it counts as too much sugar. We've included it in recipes in this book, but they all work without it.

Unacceptable:

- × **Vegetables**
- × **Fruit**
- × **Legumes**
- × **Grains**
- × **Bread**
- × **Seasonings other than salt and pepper**
- × **Sauces**
- × **Processed meats**
- × **Nuts**
- × **Seeds**
- × **Pasta**
- × **Chocolate**
- × **Alcohol**
- × **Any other non-animal-based products**

A number of people in the world have already experienced the healing power of meat! Canadian psychologist Jordan Peterson swears by the diet, and his daughter, Mikhaila, claims it has sent several of her long-term conditions into remission. This includes but is not limited to depression, severe arthritis, chronic itchiness, and lasting fatigue. Others have claimed the diet relieves joint pain, gives more energy, helps weight loss, and even kickstarts the libido!

The carnivore diet is also incredibly freeing. Unlike many diet fads, there's no set schedule or limitations on when to eat and how much. You can eat at any time of day and should eat when you are hungry and stop when you are full. Most people average around 1-2 meals a day on this method, but it's entirely down to your personal choice. Your body knows what's best for it. Your whole life, you haven't listened – but now, on the animal product diet, you can truly give it what it needs.

There's no denying that modern life is toxic. From smog in the cities to long hours stuck in cubicles, it can feel depressingly like there's no way out. But returning to the past and living as the original humans once did can give you that much-needed boost to not only feel better but approach life anew. You'll be happier, freer, healthier, and more ready to take on the world.

So, what does science have to say about all of this? Well, it'll come as no surprise to you that there's no consensus in the scientific community as of yet. Some think the diet is revolutionary, while others deny it as scurvy-causing nonsense. According to Scott

Baker, who first popularized the diet, this is due to a fear of how humanity would react if we learned that we've been malnourished this entire time!

You'll be amazed by how much your body changes after just one week of cutting non-essentials out of your diet. Sure, it might be challenging, but you'll feel like a new person so quickly you won't be able to believe it. Many people try the diet for twenty-eight or thirty days, and by the time they reach the end, they have no interest in going back.

Baker, along with many other psychologists, anthropologists, and others who support the all-animal products diet, believes that the link between our ancestors and us proves that humans achieve their optimum when on a fatty meat diet. Indeed, there is some compelling evidence to suggest such. Here are some critical scientific facts that show how we've been damaging our bodies by denying the nutrition we desperately need.

- The Human Gut
    - That's right, the very layout of our digestive tracts is a massive hint that we should be eating primarily, maybe even exclusively, meat and fats. Let's compare it with other animals. Carnivores (wolves, lions, bears, etc.) in the wild have short, uncomplex digestive tracts. In contrast, herbivores (deer, sheep, cows, etc.) have long, complex GI tracts that twist through their body as they try to break down the plant cells. Can you guess whether the human tract is more like a lion or a deer? Though a little longer than most carnivores, it's still significantly more straightforward than the herbivore gut!
- The Human Brain:
    - Our brains are enormous! So huge, in fact, that they evolved faster than childbirth could keep up. That's why our babies have such large heads, and why we spend longer in helpless infancy than many other mammals. But how do you think the brains of our ancestors got enough energy to grow? That's right – energy-rich, animal-sourced food, especially meat and fat. Without it, we wouldn't even be human as we understand it today.
- Vitamin B3 (nicotinamide or nicotinic acid)
    - The human body craves vitamin B3. Can you guess where it is mostly found? That's right – meat, eggs, and dairy products. This vitamin is responsible for brain and cell development! A vitamin B3 deficiency (or 'pellagra') has serious, often long-term effects. It can lead to brain problems like dementia, skin issues, bowel issues, and even death.
- Protein
    - Do you know how important protein is to human development? It's how every muscle and cell in your body is able to grow and get stronger. Feeling full only really happens after high-protein meals. *The Journal of Nutrition* also showed a positive effect on teens, improving their appetites

and eating habits, as well as moods and learning and understanding abilities.
- <u>Cave Paintings:</u>
  - How many cave paintings have you seen that involve loinclothed Neanderthal picking berries? How about tucking into a bowl of cereal? None? Alright, then how many can you remember where a tribe of hunters confronted a mammoth? Where a lone hunter took down a wolf or bear? The wise men of 30,000 years in our pasts only recorded what they needed – proof of the most valuable source of food to the people.
- <u>Archaeological Discoveries:</u>
  - Our archaeologists and anthropologists had uncovered animal and human bones side by side dating millions of years in our history – supposedly long before we became omnivorous. The animal bones show clear markings of smashing and cutting, meaning the animals were almost certainly slaughtered for meat, even as long ago as of this. As well, we have proof that Neanderthals relied virtually entirely on fatty meat. While early modern humans did vary their diet more – with fish, smaller mammals, and others – it was still mostly made of meat!
- <u>Vilhjalmur Stefanson</u>
  - This Arctic explorer lived for seven years with the Inuit tribes of Canada, eating nothing but meat. In 1928 this claim was tested in a hospital under intense observation. Lean meat made him feel ill, but when fattier meat was on the menu, Vilhjalmur seemed to thrive with no damage whatsoever to his body.
- <u>The Inuit Peoples</u>
  - Speaking of Inuit tribes, a study of their teeth in 1929 led to a firm conclusion that meat-only diets are the best way to keep the human mouth healthy.
- <u>"The Worst Mistake"</u>
  - Jared Diamond, the academic behind "The Worst Mistake in the History of the Human Race" (1987), described how the invention of agriculture was catastrophic to the health of humans. Common theories suggest this is because people stayed in one place for longer and became easier targets. Still, the sudden shift in diet likely led to a severe decline in health.

As you can see, none of this has come from nowhere. There's solid proof that this is the diet we're meant to be on – even if vegans and modern nutritionists would like to disagree!

There are some critical questions that you need to ask yourself before you embark on this diet. The top five are below. Think long and hard about your answers!

1. Are you able to **fully commit** to this diet?
    - This kind of diet isn't necessarily easy, at least not at first. After all, you're so used to living in a certain way that you're likely to find it very challenging to adjust to such a profound change. At first, you'll probably be very hungry, eating much more than usual.
    - It's important not to limit your calorie intake under this diet. Calorie counting is useless. The whole point of the carnivore diet is to pay attention to what you need. Eat when hungry; stop when not. If that means you eat more or less some days, that's fine.
    - Set goals and plan your shopping trips to make the whole process more comfortable for you and keep you focused.
2. **Why** are you undertaking this diet?
    - Everyone has different reasons for embarking on the carnivore diet. Some people try it for a month, some commit for longer. Some common reasons that have testified effectiveness are:
        - Weight loss
        - Energy increase/fatigue decrease
        - Treating chronic conditions
        - We are returning to our roots.
        - Relieving joint pain
    - Your reasons maybe all of these are none of them. The only important thing is that you know why you're doing this. You don't need to share it with anyone!
3. Are you ready to **eat out** on this diet?
    - It sounds like it would be difficult – but it's not really at all! Actually, you're much more likely to find options at restaurants than you would be as a vegan or keeping some other fad diet. Most restaurants will be able to set you up with a fresh steak without much issue. Obviously, you might want to avoid Chinese, Indian, and other, more seasoned foods.
4. Are you ready for the **social impact** of taking on this diet?
    - Honestly, people have too much to say about how others eat – and believe me; carnivores get some of the worst of it. Be ready for sermons from supposed 'experts' at every dinner table. Try to avoid being seated next to vegans and vegetarians.

- You might be called 'irresponsible,' 'nuts,' or even 'crazy,' even from omnivorous people. Don't let it get to you. Maybe these people would feel better if they are more meat, too!
5. Are you ready to really **listen to your body**?
    - This is much harder than you think! Years of conditioning have made us prone to what we should be doing, and not what we need to be doing.
    - Your body will tell you if it is hungry or if it is full.
    - Your body will tell you if it can or cannot tolerate certain foods (i.e., honey, milk, etc.) Only based on that will you be able to decide what sides you can use alongside the meat in your diet.
    - Your body will show you the health benefits of the diet.

Once you have these answers, you're all set to go! The following recipes are guides only. Remember, the main focus is on you! Try to source organic, grass-fed meats. If this sounds pricey, ask for the less popular cuts from your butcher. You'll be surprised at how tasty some of the bits that others leave behind can really be! Exploring all your different options and finding out what's best for you will soon leave you feeling fantastic and ready to take on anything.

So, are you ready? It's a big step, but you'll be more than grateful that you took it. Dive into these recipes, look online for more information and read, read, read! The best version of you is just around the corner. Get ready, because here you come.

Basic Recipes and Sides

Beef Broth

Prep Time: 20 mins.

Cooking Time: 8-24 hours.

Number of Servings: 1 gallon of broth

Ingredients:

8 pounds bones - preferably marrow, tails, feet, knuckles, etc.

Salt

Directions:

1. Preheat oven to 450°F.
2. Place the bones in a baking pan and roast for about 20 minutes until they turn golden brown.
3. Fill a large stockpot with 24 cups of water.
4. Put the roasted bones into the pot along with any fat and juices. If necessary, add more water so that the bones are covered.
5. Season with salt.
6. Bring the water to a gentle boil then cover the pot with the lid slightly off-center.
7. Bring the heat down to a very gentle simmer and maintain for at least 8 hours and up to 24. Do not leave unattended.
8. Scrape off any foam or film off the top.
9. If needed, add water to make sure the bones remain covered. It becomes better the longer you cook it.
10. Remove from the heat and allow the broth to cool.
11. Using a mesh or cheesecloth, strain the broth and store it in a container.
12. It can last for up to 5 days in the fridge and up to 6 months in the freezer.

Nutritional Values (Per Serving):
Calories: 17
Fat: 0.4g
Saturated Fat: 0.3g
Trans Fat: 0g
Carbohydrates: 0g
Fiber: 0g

Sodium: 893mg
Protein: 2.7g

Tallow and Cracklings

Prep Time: 25 mins, plus 2 hr. chilling time

Cooking Time: 3-4 hours

Ingredients:

6lb Grass-fed Beef suet

Directions:

1. Chill your suet for a couple of hours so it will become easier to slice.
2. Start by cutting the suet into tiny pieces. The smaller the parts, the easier the fat will be extracted. If you wish, you may use a food processor to do it. Make sure to cut the larger pieces anyway, so it doesn't clog your machine.
3. Start pulsing the suet until it looks crumbled. If the processor clogs, remove some of the pieces and blend again. You may need to run multiple batches.
4. Add the ground suet to a stockpot over low heat. Do not add water.
5. Keep the heat very low so as to melt the fat but not burn it and keep checking the pot hourly, stirring so that it doesn't stick.
6. The process may take from 3-5 hours, depending on the size of the pieces, the pot you're using, and the intensity of your stove.
7. You can tell the tallow is done cooking when the suet begins to shrink into tiny and shriveled pieces.
8. Strain the liquid fat, let it slightly cool, then store in a clean and dry (preferably sterilized) jar. You may also use a silicone mold to make butter-like chunks of tallow.
9. You can eat the cracklings too after they cool!

Nutritional Values (Per Tablespoon):

Calories: 115
Fat: 12.8g
Saturated Fat: 6.4g
Trans Fat: 0.5g
Carbohydrates: 0g
Fiber: 0g
Sodium: 0mg
Protein: 0g

Carnivore "Bread"

Prep Time: 15 mins.

Cooking Time: 20 mins.

Number of Servings: Around 16 squares

Ingredients:

9oz cream cheese

3 free-range eggs

12oz fatty bacon, cooked

6.5oz cheddar cheese, grated

1/3 cup parmesan cheese

Directions:

1. Chop the cooked bacon as small and possible. Use a food processor if you like.
2. In a blender, add the cream cheese and the eggs and blend.
3. Add the bacon in the mixture and blend some more.
4. Fold in the rest of the cheeses.
5. Line a baking sheet with parchment paper.
6. Using a spatula, spread the mixture on the baking sheet laying it as flat as possible.
7. Bake at 390F for around 20 minutes.
8. Eat as a side, cut into portions, or use it as a carnivore pizza base!

Nutritional Values (Per Serving):

Calories: 229
Fat: 18.3g
Saturated Fat: 8.4g
Trans Fat: 2g
Carbohydrates: 0g
Fiber: 0g
Sodium: 643mg
Protein: 14.5g

Livers in a Blanket

Prep Time: 10 mins.

Cooking Time: 12 minutes

Number of Servings: 16 pieces

Ingredients:

2lbs grass-fed venison liver

16 slices of fatty bacon

Salt

Directions:

1. Preheat your oven to 390F
2. Cut the liver into 16 pieces, around 1 inch thick each.
3. Wrap the bacon around the liver and pin it with a toothpick to secure
4. Salt to taste
5. Bake until crispy, around 12 minutes
6. Don't forget to take out the toothpicks before serving!

Nutritional Values (Per Serving):

Calories: 178
Fat: 9.9g
Saturated Fat: 3.4g
Trans Fat: 0.1g
Carbohydrates: 0g
Fiber: 0g
Sodium: 625mg
Protein: 18.5g

Crispy Skin Chips

Prep Time: 10 mins.

Cooking Time: 30 mins.

Number of Servings: 8

Ingredients:

2 pounds of chicken skin

Salt

Directions:

1. Prepare a sheet pan with wax paper.
2. Preheat your oven to 330F
3. Cut skins into strips or squares according to your preference.
4. Season with salt to taste
5. Arrange skins on the sheet. It's okay if the skins touch as they will shrink while roasting.
6. Take another wax paper and place it over the skins then cover it with a second baking sheet. This will make lovely and flat chips.
7. Bake for about 15 minutes.
8. Flip the skins over and bake for an additional 15 minutes.
9. Let the chips cool before you eat them.

Nutritional Values (Per Serving):

Calories: 572
Fat: 51.2g
Saturated Fat: 14.4g
Trans Fat: 0.5g
Carbohydrates: 0g
Fiber: 0g
Sodium: 82mg
Protein: 25.7g

Beef Pâté

Prep Time: 10 mins.

Cooking Time: 10 mins+ 4-5 hours to chill.

Number of Servings: 12

Ingredients:

1lb beef liver

12 Tbsp tallow, divided

1 teaspoon salt

1 teaspoon ground black pepper

1/2 cup high-fat heavy cream (optional)

Directions:

1. In a skillet, melt 6 tablespoons of the tallow.
2. Slice the liver into thin strips and add to the skillet.
3. Sprinkle with salt and cook for a minute on each side of the strip.
4. Let the liver cool for around 5 minutes.
5. Add the liver in a blender and pulse until it's smooth.
6. Add the remaining tallow and the cream if you're using it.
7. Add salt to taste and blend until all ingredients are combined into a smooth paste.
8. Remove from the blender and place in an airtight glass container.
9. Let it chill for at least 4 hours to harden.
10. Enjoy!

Nutritional Values (Per Serving):

Calories: 216
Fat: 18.3g
Saturated Fat: 9.2g
Trans Fat: 0.8g

Carbohydrates: 0g
Fiber: 0g
Sodium: 287mg
Protein: 10.2g

Liver Chips

Prep Time: 10 mins.

Cooking Time: 7-8 hours

Number of Servings: 32

Ingredients:

2lbs rudiment liver (Beef, lamb, etc.), ground

Directions:

1. In your food processor or blender, blend the minced liver until it resembles a paste.
2. Line a baking sheet with wax paper and spread the liver paste on it evenly using a spatula. Try to make it as thin as possible. Do it in two batches if needed.
3. Set your oven at the lowest possible temperature. This is usually 120F.
4. Once the center is dry (around 3 hours depending on your oven), flip the liver around and leave it to keep cooking.
5. Keep checking on it after the 6th (out of 8) hour mark. It's ready when the edges begin to separate, and the liver has dried.
6. Break into pieces and store in an airtight container.

Nutritional Values (Per Serving):

Calories: 34
Fat: 2g
Saturated Fat: 2g
Trans Fat: 0g
Carbohydrates: 0g
Fiber: 0g
Sodium: 26mg
Protein: 6g

Salmon Skin Chips

Prep Time: 20 mins.

Cooking Time: 15 mins.

Number of Servings: 4

Ingredients:

Skin from 4 salmons or other fish of your choice

1/3 cup ghee

Salt

Directions:

1. Preheat your oven to 395F
2. Prepare a sheet pan with wax paper.
3. Separate the skins from the fish using a sharp knife, or ask for the skin separated when you purchase it.
4. If there's any leftover fish flesh on the skin, separate it with a spoon to make sure the skins will be absolutely crispy.
5. Cut the skins into 2-inch pieces.
6. Arrange skins on the sheet, making sure they are skin face-down and that they don't touch
7. Using a kitchen brush, brush the skins with ghee.
8. Season with salt to taste.
9. Take another wax paper and place it over the skins then cover it with a second baking sheet. This will make lovely and flat chips and ensure that the fish skin won't bubble as much.
10. Bake for approximately 15 minutes.
11. Using a spatula, remove the fish skins from the tray and serve them on a plate

Nutritional Values (Per Serving):

Calories: 408
Fat: 33.6g
Saturated Fat: 19.3g

Trans Fat: 1g
Carbohydrates: 4g
Fiber: 0g
Sodium: 842mg
Protein: 21g

Wrapped Hearts

Prep Time: 15 mins.

Cooking Time: 15 mins

Number of Servings: 24 pieces

Ingredients:

3lbs grass-fed beef heart, cleaned with arteries removed

24 slices of fatty bacon

24 slices cheddar

Salt

Directions:

1. Preheat your oven to 390F
2. Wash the heart and make sure any arteries are cut out.
3. Slice in half then cut into 24 pieces, around 1 inch thick each.
4. Wrap the bacon and cheddar around the heart pieces and pin it with a toothpick to secure
5. Salt to taste
6. Bake until crispy, around 15 minutes
7. Don't forget to take out the toothpicks before serving!

Nutritional Values (Per Serving):

Calories: 309
Fat: 19.9g
Saturated Fat: 9.3g
Trans Fat: 1g
Carbohydrates: 0g
Fiber: 0g
Sodium: 646mg
Protein: 30.2g

Shrimp Stuffing

Prep Time: 15 mins.

Cooking Time: 60 mins.

Number of Servings: 6

Ingredients:

6 tbsp ghee

1/2 cup chicken livers, chopped

1 lb. shrimp, clean and deveined

1 tbsp parmesan flakes

1 1/2 cup carnivore "bread" crumbs

1 cup full-fat milk

1 tbsp beef gelatin

3/4 cup grated cheddar cheese

Sprinkles of red pepper

salt to taste

Directions:

1. In a large pan, add 3 tablespoons of ghee over medium-high heat. Sauté the livers until they're tender
2. Add the shrimp and keep cooking until they turn nice and pink.
3. Add the parmesan cheese and remove from heat.
4. Add the crumbs and mix very well.
5. Take another pan and add the rest of the ghee and melt if hardened.
6. Reduce the heat then add the milk and gelatin, stirring until thickened.
7. Add the cheddar cheese and remove from the heat.
8. Whisk continuously until the cheese melts and combines
9. Pour this mixture over the shrimp mixture and stir so that they mix well.
10. Transfer to a baking dish and cover with tin foil.
11. Bake for about 35 minutes, then uncover and bake for another 10 minutes.

12. Make sure it is room temperature before you stuff your bird.

Nutritional Values (Per Serving):

Calories: 428
Fat: 30.5g
Saturated Fat: 13.7g
Trans Fat: 1g
Carbohydrates: 0g
Fiber: 0g
Sodium: 1045mg
Protein: 33.1g

Carn "Bread" Stuffing

Prep Time: 15 mins.

Cooking Time: 55 mins.

Number of Servings: 12

Ingredients:

2 tbsp tallow

4 cups carnivore "bread" crumbled

1/2lb chicken livers, chopped

1/2lb chicken gizzards, chopped

Salt and pepper to taste

Chicken broth

Directions:

1. For stuffing, it's best to use dried "bread." If you don't have any at hand, you can dice fresh "bread" then put it in the for about 10 minutes at 300°F
2. You can make the stuffing ahead of time and store it in the fridge for up to 48 hours to use it when you need it. However, it should be at room temperature before you can use it.
3. Preheat your oven to 350°F.
4. In a large pan, melt your tallow over medium heat. Add the livers and gizzards and sauté until tender, about 15 minutes.
5. In a bowl, place your "bread" cubes. Season with salt and pepper
6. Pour broth on the "bread" until they're moistened but not soggy.
7. Transfer both "bread" and meats in a baking dish and cover with tin foil.
8. Bake for about 35 minutes, then uncover and bake for another 10 minutes.
9. Make sure it is room temperature before you stuff your bird.

Nutritional Values (Per Serving):

Calories: 320
Fat: 22.3g
Saturated Fat: 12.4g

Trans Fat: 2g
Carbohydrates: 0g
Fiber: 0g
Sodium: 1643mg
Protein: 20.5g

Carni Protein Bar

Prep Time: 20 mins.

Cooking Time: 5 mins+time to set

Number of Servings: 24

Ingredients:

2 pounds lamb mince, dried (you may also use other kinds of meat or tallow such as venison, elk, beef, etc.)

Salt

2 pounds tallow

Directions:

1. Melt the tallow in a double-boiler or a microwave-safe bowl.
2. In a separate bowl, mix the meat and the salt.
3. Star pouring the tallow on the meat. Make sure it's not too hot.
4. Start stirring, so they combine well. The tallow should be enough to make the meat moist throughout but shouldn't pool.
5. If the mixture is too dry, you can add more tallow.
6. You can let the mix set in a baking dish or use muffin liners to separate portions. You can even form it into balls with your hands!

Nutritional Values (Per Serving):

Calories: 404
Fat: 39.2g
Saturated Fat: 19.5g
Trans Fat: 2g
Carbohydrates: 0g
Fiber: 2g
Sodium: 1053mg
Protein: 11.7g

Breakfast

Carnaffles

Prep Time: 15 mins.

Cooking Time: 5 mins.

Number of Servings: 4

Ingredients:

8oz grass-fed ground beef

5 duck eggs

Tallow or Ghee

Raw honey as a topping (optional)

Directions:

1. In a saucepan, add the meat and cover it with water. Bring to a gentle boil, then let it simmer for about 10-15 mins or until the meat changes color.
2. Strain the water and keep it as the fat of the meat will separate when cooking with water.
3. Put the strained water in the freezer until the fat rises to the top, then skim the fat off and add it back to the meat.
4. Heat your waffle iron.
5. Transfer the meat in a blender, then add the eggs in and blend until it combines in a smooth batter.
6. Use the tallow to grease your waffle iron.
7. Pour enough batter for a waffle onto your iron and cook until ready.
8. Repeat until you use up all the batter
9. Serve plain or top with butter (high fat low lactose) or honey.

Nutritional Values (Per Serving):

Calories: 340
Fat: 26.9g

Saturated Fat: 10.8g
Polyunsaturated Fat: 1.3 g
Monounsaturated Fat: 8.4 g
Carbohydrates: 0g
Fiber: 0g
Sodium: 299.9 mg
Protein: 21.7 g

Eggs and Bacon Breakfast Meat Sandwich

Prep Time: 10 mins.

Cooking Time: 10 mins.

Number of Servings: 2 sandwiches

Ingredients:

6oz ground beef

Salt

3 eggs

2oz cheddar cheese (or other high fat low lactose cheese)

1 tsp tallow or bacon grease

2 slices of fatty bacon

Directions:

1. In a bowl, mix the meat with 1 egg and salt to taste until well combined.
2. Form the mixture into four patties about half an inch thick each
3. Get a non-stick skillet, let it get very hot, then melt your tallow and add the patties.
4. Cook until they are well-done and brown, around 3 minutes, then flip and repeat.
5. When the patties are done, cook the bacon slices until crispy.
6. Use the same pan to incorporate all the right flavors and cook the two eggs sunny side up. If you like a moist sandwich, keep the yolk runny.

For each sandwich:

7. Using a spatula, put one patty on a dish that will serve as the bottom "bun."
8. Top with one slice of bacon, cheese, and one egg then finish with another patty.

Nutritional Values (Per Serving):

Calories: 1134
Fat: 87.5g
Saturated Fat: 36.3g
Trans Fat: 10g

Carbohydrates: 0g
Fiber: 0g
Sodium: 809mg
Protein: 83g

Carni Muffins

Prep Time: 6 mins.

Cooking Time: 20 mins.

Number of Servings: 12

Ingredients:

2lbs grass-fed venison, ground

2lbs grass-fed venison liver, ground

2 tsp salt

Directions:

1. Line a muffin tin with muffin liners.
2. Preheat your oven at 350F.
3. In a bowl, combine the two kinds of ground meat and mix until they're well incorporated.
4. Add salt to taste.
5. Divide the dough evenly among the 12 liners.
6. Bake for around 20 minutes.

Nutritional Values (Per Serving):

Calories: 491
Fat: 26.1g
Saturated Fat: 10.1g
Trans Fat: 1.2g
Carbohydrates: 0g
Fiber: 0g
Sodium: 758mg
Protein: 60.1g

Carncakes

Prep Time: 35 mins.

Cooking Time: 4 mins.

Number of Servings: 8

Ingredients:

1lb free-range chicken, ground

10 eggs

Ghee for the skillet

1 cup heavy cream for topping, whipped (optional)

Directions:

1. In a saucepan, add the meat and cover it with water. Bring to a gentle boil, then let it simmer for about 30 mins or until the meat changes color.
2. Heat a non-stick skillet until it gets very hot.
3. Transfer the meat in a blender, then add the eggs in and blend until it combines in a smooth batter.
4. Use the ghee to grease your skillet.
5. Pour enough batter for a pancake in your skillet and cook until it bubbles, then flips to the other side, about 2 minutes on each side.
6. Repeat until you use up all the batter
7. Serve plain or top with butter (high fat low lactose) and whipped cream.

Nutritional Values (Per Serving):

Calories: 411
Fat: 19g
Saturated Fat: 6.4g
Trans Fat: 0.4 g
Carbohydrates: 0g
Fiber: 0g

Sodium: 207 mg
Protein: 55.7 g

Fish muffins

Prep Time: 30 mins.

Cooking Time: 15 mins.

Number of Servings: 12

Ingredients:

16oz cod

16oz salmon fillet

8oz ghee

1 egg

5oz parmesan cheese

2 tsp salt

2tsp pepper

Directions:

1. Line a muffin tin with muffin liners
2. Preheat your oven at 350F.
3. Cut the cod and salmon into tiny chunks and transfer to your food processor or blender.
4. Blend until they're well incorporated.
5. Add the cheese and egg to the mixture and mix with a spoon.
6. Add salt and pepper to taste.
7. Using a spoon, divide the dough among the liners.
8. Bake for around 15-20 minutes.

Nutritional Values (Per Serving):

Calories: 299
Fat: 24.4g
Saturated Fat: 13.9g

Trans Fat: 1.2g
Carbohydrates: 0g
Fiber: 0g
Sodium: 549mg
Protein: 20.3g

Lamb Scotch Eggs

Prep Time: 15 mins.

Cooking Time: 20 mins.

Number of Servings: 6

Ingredients:

1lb lamb sausage meat, ground

6 large hard-boiled eggs, peeled

Salt to taste

Directions:

1. Preheat your oven to 350F
2. In a bowl, mix the meat with the salt and knead until thoroughly combined
3. Form 6 balls with your hands. Try to make them the same size.
4. Line a rimmed baking dish with wax paper
5. Arrange the balls on the dish and press flat. Use a rolling pin if necessary.
6. In each meat disc, place an egg.
7. Carefully wrap the meat around the eggs, making sure they are entirely covered without holes.
8. Place in the oven and bake for about 10 minutes or until the top side looks cooked.
9. Flip and bake the other side until crispy.
10. Serve hot

Nutritional Values (Per Serving):

Calories: 280
Fat: 21.6g
Saturated Fat: 9.1g
Trans Fat: 0.8g
Carbohydrates: 0.1g
Fiber: 0g
Sodium: 1203mg
Protein: 18g

Meatballs Surprise

Prep Time: 5 mins.

Cooking Time: 20 mins.

Number of Servings: 8

Ingredients:

16oz grass-fed beef, ground

16oz grass-fed beef heart, ground

2 tsp salt

Directions:

1. Line a 16x16 baking dish with wax paper
2. Preheat your oven at 350F.
3. In a bowl, combine the two kinds of ground meat and mix until they're well incorporated.
4. Add salt to taste.
5. Using a scoop, take enough dough and form it into a ball by rolling it with your hands.
6. Place onto the prepared dish and repeat until you run out of dough.
7. Bake for around 20 minutes.
8. The meatballs will ooze out their juices while baking. Save it and serve it over the warm meatballs as a "sauce."

Nutritional Values (Per Serving):

Calories: 481
Fat: 25.1g
Saturated Fat: 10.3g
Trans Fat: 1g
Carbohydrates: 0g
Fiber: 0g
Sodium: 797mg
Protein: 59.1g

Offal Pie

Prep Time: 5 mins.

Cooking Time: 20 mins.

Number of Servings: 8

Ingredients:

1lb goat meat, ground

1/2 goat lungs, ground

1lb goat liver, ground

1lb goat heart, ground

6 eggs

Tallow, melted

Salt

Directions:

1. Preheat your oven to 350F
2. Grease a pie dish with tallow
3. In a bowl, add all of your meats, then add the eggs. Knead thoroughly until evenly combined.
4. Season with salt
5. Combine all ingredients in a mixing bowl. Salt to taste.
6. Transfer the mixture into the pie dish
7. Bake for about 20 minutes
8. Take it out of the oven and let it slightly cool before serving.
9. It can be eaten warm or cold.

Nutritional Values (Per Serving):

Calories: 450
Fat: 17.9g
Saturated Fat: 6.8g
Trans Fat: 0.1g
Carbohydrates: 0g

Fiber: 0g
Sodium: 146mg
Protein: 64g

Bacon Cups

Prep Time: 5 mins.

Cooking Time: 20 mins.

Number of Servings: 12

Ingredients:

12 slices bacon

12 eggs

Salt & pepper to taste

1/2 cup cheddar cheese, shredded

Directions:

1. Preheat your oven to 400F
2. Line a muffin tin with muffin liners
3. Arrange the bacon slices in the liners, making a circle with each one
4. Put in the oven for around 10 minutes
5. Take out of the oven and crack one egg in each muffin slot in the center of the bacon circle
6. Season with salt and pepper to taste then top with the cheese
7. Bake for another 10 minutes.
8. Serve immediately

Nutritional Values (Per Serving):

Calories: 365
Fat: 32.9g
Saturated Fat: 11.3g
Trans Fat: 1g
Carbohydrates: 0g
Fiber: 0g
Sodium: 541mg
Protein: 15.3g

Eggs in a Basket

Prep Time: 10 mins.

Cooking Time: 25 mins.

Number of Servings: 8

Ingredients:

2lb grass-fed beef, ground

Salt

Pepper

4 tbsp tallow

8 eggs

8 slices cheddar cheese

8 slices bacon, cooked

Directions:

1. Form the beef into 6 patties
2. Using a shot glass, cut a hole in the middle of each patty like a ring shape
3. Use the excess meat to form two additional patties and also cut out the centers
4. Season with salt and pepper to taste
5. Melt the tallow in a large non-stick pan over high heat
6. Place the patties in the pan and cook for two minutes
7. Flip and crack an egg in the middle of the ring
8. Season egg with salt and pepper then cover the pan and let it cook until the egg white is set, about 5 minutes
9. Remove from heat and take off the lid
10. top each basket with a cheddar slice, then replace the lid to allow the cheese to melt
11. Finish with a crispy bacon slice on top

Nutritional Values (Per Serving):

Calories: 388
Fat: 34.1g

Saturated Fat: 14g
Trans Fat: 0.2g
Carbohydrates: 0g
Fiber: 0g
Sodium: 472mg
Protein: 18.4g

Lunch & Dinner

Cheesy Wings

Prep Time: 10 mins.

Cooking Time: 60 mins.

Number of Servings: 4

Ingredients:

2 pounds of chicken wings

1/4 cup parmesan grated

1/2 tsp salt

1/2 tsp ground black pepper

1/8 cup ghee

Directions:

1. Preheat your oven to 350F
2. Prepare a baking sheet by lining it with wax paper.
3. In a wide microwave-safe bowl, melt the ghee.
4. In a separate bowl, mix the parmesan cheese, the salt, and the pepper.
5. Dip each wing in the fat and then in the cheese mix bowl until they're well-covered.
6. Set on the baking sheet and repeat until you have done the same to all wings.
7. Bake until they're nicely crispy, about an hour.
8. Serve warm.

Nutritional Values (Per Serving):

Calories: 398
Fat: 36g
Saturated Fat: 15g
Trans Fat: 1g
Carbohydrates: 0g

Fiber: 0g
Sodium: 531mg
Protein: 25g

Grilled Shrimp

Prep Time: 20 mins.

Cooking Time: 5 mins.

Number of Servings: 2

Ingredients:

1/2lb jumbo shrimp, deveined and peeled

Salt and pepper for seasoning

1/2 cup ghee

Directions:

1. Season the shrimp with salt
2. Combine all other ingredients in a bowl
3. Leave the shrimp in the mixture to marinate. It needs at least one hour but is better overnight
4. Turn on your grill and bring it to medium-high heat
5. Thread skewers through the shrimp and place on grill.
6. Turn on your grill and bring it to medium-high heat.
7. Grill for about 3-5 mins until no longer pink, flipping halfway through.

Nutritional Values (Per Serving):

Calories: 341
Fat: 27g
Saturated Fat: 3g
Sodium 1354mg
Trans Fat: 0g
Carbohydrates: 2g
Fiber: 1.5g

Lengua Carnitas

Prep Time: 5 mins.

Cooking Time: 8 hours.

Number of Servings: 8

Ingredients:

2lbs Grass-fed beef tongue (1 tongue)

Sea Salt

Directions:

1. Heavily season the tongue with salt and place in a crockpot
2. Cover the tongue with water.
3. Set the heat on low and let the tongue cook for about 8 hours or until the tongue is tender. You should be able to poke through it easily.
4. Save the broth for later.
5. Let the tongue to cool.
6. When the tongue is cool enough to handle, slit the skin a little with sears or a knife then begin peeling it off with your hands.
7. Using two forks, scrape on the tongue's surface, so it shreds and starts looking like pulled meat.
8. Use the desired amount of broth as a sauce and to keep the meat moist.
9. Enjoy!

Nutritional Values (Per Serving):

Calories: 253
Fat: 18g
Saturated Fat: 8g
Trans Fat: 1g
Carbohydrates: 0g
Fiber: 0g
Sodium: 78mg
Protein: 17g

Sea Bass in Paper

Prep Time: 15 mins.

Cooking Time: 15 mins.

Number of Servings: 4

Ingredients:

2lb sea bass, filleted

Salt

Pepper

2 tablespoon grass-fed butter

Directions:

1. Preheat your oven to 350F
2. Line a baking dish with wax paper and place the sea bass, skin side down on it
3. Season the fillets with salt and pepper to taste
4. Make sure the fillets are a little lower than the center of the paper, then add a tbsp of butter on each
5. Lightly water the edges of the paper fold into a packet
6. Bake for 10-15 minutes.
7. Serve hot.

Nutritional Values (Per Serving):

Calories: 324
Fat: 9g
Saturated Fat: 3g
Trans Fat: 0g
Carbohydrates: 27g
Fiber: 0g
Sodium: 560mg
Protein: 56g

Oxtail Stew

Prep Time: 20 mins.

Cooking Time: 60 mins.

Number of Servings: 6

Ingredients:

3-4lbs oxtail

Salt

Pepper

½ pint beef broth

4 tbsp lard or other animal fat of your preference

You will also need a pressure cooker

Directions:

1. In a skillet over high heat, place the oxtail, 4 tbsps. of lard, salt, and pepper to taste
2. Sauté for 3 minutes on either side or until it becomes golden brown.
3. Place the meat in a pressure cooker and set it over medium-high heat.
4. Add the broth and close the lid.
5. Turn the valve to the proper pressure indicator and let the meat simmer on low heat for 60 minutes.
6. Serve with pepper, salt, and lard.

Nutritional Values (Per Serving):

Calories: 391
Fat: 24g
Saturated Fat: 8.5g
Trans Fat: 0.9g
Carbohydrates: 0g
Fiber: 0g
Sodium: 235mg
Protein: 38g

Patsa

Prep Time: 30 mins.

Cooking Time: 2 hours.

Number of Servings: 4

Ingredients:

1 beef shank, cleaned and cut into pieces

1 beef belly, cleaned and cut into pieces

Water

1 tbsp Tallow

Salt and pepper to taste

Directions:

1. It's better if you ask your butcher to clean and cut the shank and belly, but if you have experience with it, you may also do this yourself
2. Wash the meat thoroughly and place in a pot
3. Pour in water until it covers the beef halfway
4. Add the tallow and bring it to a boil, letting it cook for about an hour.
5. Remove from heat
6. Using a skimming spoon, remove the pieces of meat and let them cool. Leave the broth in the pot.
7. When the meat cools enough to handle, pull it off the bones and then cut all parts into small pieces
8. Place back into the pot and season with salt and pepper to taste.
9. Cover the pot with a lid and boil for another hour.
10. Serve hot with more tallow if you like.

Nutritional Values (Per 1 Cup):

Calories: 177
Fat: 8.3g
Saturated Fat: 4.1g

Trans Fat: 0.3g
Carbohydrates: 0g
Fiber: 0g
Sodium: 827mg
Protein: 17g

Turkish Kokoreç

Prep Time: 60 minutes + 90 minutes hands off

Cooking Time: 2 hrs. 30 minutes.

Number of Servings: 8

Ingredients:

4lbs lamb intestines, thoroughly cleaned

Salt

1 lamb caul fat

1 lamb pluck including sweetbreads

Pepper

You will also need

A 12x16 baking tray fitted with a rack

Two 12" steel skewers

Directions:

1. Wash intestines thoroughly inside and out.
2. In a large bowl, add 2oz of water and 2 tbsp of salt.
3. Let the intestines soak for 10 minutes, then rinse
4. Drain and discard water, then place intestines in a bowl and let it chill in the refrigerator for about 2 hours.
5. In a separate bowl, add the caul fat and rinse thoroughly using warm water.
6. Let pluck soak in the water for 30 minutes.
7. Drain and set aside.
8. While the caul fat soaks, wash the lamb pluck thoroughly
9. Chop into small pieces around 2" thick
10. Place in a bowl and sprinkle with pepper. Do not add salt yet as it will toughen the meat.
11. Let it marinate for 1 hour.
12. Preheat oven to 390F on the Fan setting.

13. Take one skewer and begin threading the pluck in the following order lungs, heart, liver, sweetbreads, keep going in the same order until you're out.
14. Season with salt and pepper to taste.
15. Take the caul fat and cat a large enough piece to cover the whole skewer and nicely wrap it around the meats.
16. Begin wrapping the intestines around the meat. Cover the whole skewer and tie it up at the edge of the skewer. The process is quite time-consuming and will need a lot of intestines!
17. Using wax paper, wrap the skewer then cover again with tin foil
18. Transfer to the tray
19. Roast for 2 hours, then remove the tin foil and paper.
20. Roast again until golden, approximately 30 minutes.
21. Serve hot, seasoned with salt and pepper to taste.

Nutritional Values (Per Serving):

Calories: 490
Fat: 24g
Saturated Fat: 11g
Trans Fat: 1g
Carbohydrates: 0g
Fiber: 0g
Sodium: 242mg
Protein: 61g

Greek Magiritsa

Prep Time: 25 mins.

Cooking Time: 5 mins.

Number of Servings: 8

Ingredients:

2lbs lamb pluck, cleaned

1/2lb lamb intestines, cleaned

Salt

1 tbsp black pepper

4-5 tablespoons tallow

2 pints water

1 pint+ 2 fl oz beef broth

For the egg finish:

2 eggs

salt

pepper

Directions:

1. Fill a pot with water and set over high heat.
2. Bring to a boil then add the lamb pluck, intestines, salt, and pepper.
3. Let it boil for about 15 minutes, skimming the foam off the top often.
4. Drain the water and discard it. Let the meats cool.
5. When cooled, finely chop them in small pieces.
6. Return the pot to high heat and add the tallow.
7. Add the meats in the pot and sauté for 8-10 minutes.
8. Deglaze with the 2fl oz of broth then add the rest of the broth and the water
9. Cover the pot with a lid and let it boil over medium heat for about an hour.

For the egg finish:

10. In a bowl, add the eggs, salt, and pepper and whisk until the egg froths slightly.
11. Slowly add 5-6 ladlefuls of the hot stock, whisking continuously, so the egg doesn't cook.
12. When you feel the bowl becoming warm, add the mixture in the pot.
13. Shake the pot so that it distributes evenly and remove from the heat.
14. Season with salt and pepper to taste.
15. Serve with tallow and black pepper.

Nutritional Values (Per Serving):

Calories: 300
Fat: 12g
Saturated Fat: 4g
Trans Fat: 0g
Carbohydrates: 0g
Fiber: 0g
Sodium: 712mg
Protein: 26g

Pork Belly Fry

Prep Time: 30 mins.

Cooking Time: 10 mins.

Number of Servings: 6

Ingredients:

2lb pork belly, boneless

2-3 tablespoons lard

Salt

Pepper

1-2 tsp beef or chicken broth

Directions:

1. Cut the pork belly into small ¼ inch cubes.
2. Place the meat in a bowl and add the lard, salt, and pepper.
3. Mix well to coat the pieces evenly and set aside to marinate
4. Place a large skillet over high heat and leave it to get very hot.
5. Add the pork belly to the skillet and let it cook until it is crispy and golden, about 3 minutes on each side.
6. Don't stir much to ensure the meat cooks properly and doesn't boil.
7. Deglaze with 1-2tsp of broth and mix.
8. If your skillet isn't big enough, you can do this in two batches.
9. Serve with salt and pepper to taste on their own or on carnivore "bread" pieces.

Nutritional Values (Per Serving):

Calories: 756
Fat: 47.1g
Saturated Fat: 20g
Trans Fat: 2g
Carbohydrates: 0g
Fiber: 0g
Sodium: 2458mg
Protein: 69.g

Goat Stew

Prep Time: 20 mins.

Cooking Time: 60 mins.

Number of Servings: 8

Ingredients:

4 lbs. goat, with bone

4-5 tbsp tallow

Salt

Pepper

2 pints of chicken broth

To serve:

Parmesan cheese, grated

You will also need a pressure cooker

Directions:

1. Set the pressure cooker over high heat and add 2 tablespoons tallow.
2. In a bowl, place the goat meat along with 2-3 tablespoons tallow and season with salt and pepper to taste. Coat evenly.
3. Place in the pressure cooker and sauté on both sides until golden brown.
4. Add the broth and close with the lid.
5. Turn the valve to the proper indicator and let the meat boil over medium-low heat for about 50 minutes.
6. Serve with plenty of broth and grated parmesan cheese over it.

Nutritional Values (Per Serving):

Calories: 488
Fat: 19g
Saturated Fat: 7.7g

Trans Fat: 0.8g
Carbohydrates: 0g
Fiber: 0g
Sodium: 253mg
Protein: 47g

Pork Pockets with Cheese and Bacon

Prep Time: 30 mins.

Cooking Time: 20 mins.

Number of Servings: 4

Ingredients:

4 thick pork steaks

7oz cheddar cheese

8 slices bacon

4 tablespoons lard

2 tablespoons beef stock

To serve:

Parmesan, grated

Directions:

1. Preheat your oven to 390F on the fan setting.
2. Place a skillet over high heat.
3. Score the steak at several points on the fat over the bone.
4. Make a pocket on the fleshy part for the stuffing.
5. Cut the bacon and the cheddar into thin slices and divide between the steaks. Secure the pocket with a toothpick.
6. Brush the steaks with a bit of lard then place vertically on the skillet, making sure the fat touches the pan. Cook until it's golden brown.
7. Cook on either side until they're golden brown, about 4 minutes.
8. Brush half the stock on one side, then transfer to a baking dish with a rack. Place the unbrushed side up.
9. Brush the rest of the stock on the other side of the steaks.
10. Bake for about 20 minutes.
11. Serve with grated parmesan

Nutritional Values (Per Serving):

Calories: 1420

Fat: 75g
Saturated Fat: 25g
Trans Fat: 0g
Carbohydrates: 0g
Fiber: 0g
Sodium: 1762mg
Protein: 66g

Spit-Roast Lamb

Prep Time: 55 mins.

Cooking Time: 5 hours.

Number of Servings: 16

Ingredients:

Ingredients

20lbs lamb (1 lamb)

5oz salt

1tbsp pepper

5oz kefalotyri cheese

7oz tallow, melted

Directions:

1. Place the lamb on a clean table and season inside and out with some salt and pepper.
2. Insert the skewer through the back of the lamb all across the spine until you reach the skull's base.
3. Rotate the head so you can pass the skewer under the eyes.
4. Use a pair of spit forks to prick the lamb's legs, so it retains its balance on the spit.
5. Using a stainless steel wire, wrap the lamb along the hips, rack, and neck, then pass it through the lamb and tie it securely on the spit.
6. Follow up with tying the legs and neck on the skewer as well.
7. Place the kefalotyri cheese on the inside of the lamb, cut into pieces.
8. Using kitchen twine and a thick needle, sew the stomach of the lamb.
9. Brush tallow on the outside of the lamb and further season with salt and pepper
10. In a bowl, add the remaining tallow and keep warm so that it stays melted.
11. Place the spit in the highest position and roast for around 5 hours.
12. Lower the spit every hour.
13. Make sure to baste the lamb every 15 minutes with the melted tallow.
14. Ideally, the majority of the charcoal should be under the legs and back of the lamb.

15. Serve hot.

Nutritional Values (Per Serving):

Calories: 270
Fat: 30g
Saturated Fat: 10g
Trans Fat: 1g
Carbohydrates: 0g
Fiber: 0g
Sodium: 400mg
Protein: 21g

Butter Quail

Prep Time: 10 mins.

Cooking Time: 30 mins.

Number of Servings: 4

Ingredients:

2 tablespoons grass-fed butter (or other fat of your preference)

8 quails

salt

pepper

1 cup of water

Directions:

1. Season the quails with salt and pepper to taste
2. In a deep skillet or wok, heat the butter over medium heat.
3. Sauté the quails for 3 minutes with the breast side down.
4. Flip them over.
5. Deglaze with water, then cover the skillet and let it simmer for about 10 minutes.
6. Set the quails on a plate and keep them warm.
7. Continue simmering the broth in the pan until it resembles a thick sauce.
8. Serve with the broth over the quails.

Nutritional Values (Per Serving):

Calories: 470
Fat: 32g
Saturated Fat: 11g
Trans Fat: 1g
Carbohydrates: 0g
Fiber: 0g
Sodium: 197mg
Protein: 42.9g

Full Carnivore Turducken Masterpiece

Prep Time: 2 hours.

Cooking Time: 5 hours.

Number of Servings: 20

Ingredients:

1 whole turkey, boned, with wings and legs still intact ~ 25lbs

1 whole duck, boned ~6lbs

1 whole chicken, boned ~3lbs

Kitchen twine and a large thick needle

1 lb. ground beef

2 cups beef broth

<u>Carn "bread" stuffing</u>

<u>Shrimp stuffing</u>

Directions:

1. Ask your butcher to bone the birds unless you are experienced in doing it yourself. Make sure to ask for the turkey's wings and legs to be left intact.
2. Ideally, you can prepare the stuffings at an earlier time so that they're at room temperature when you need to stuff the birds.
3. Begin by lightly cooking the ground beef in the 2 cups of broth until it absorbs the liquid and resembles stuffing
4. Preheat your oven to 325F

To assemble:

5. Each layer of stuffing should be about 1/2 inch thick.
6. Place the turkey on your worktop with the skin-side-down. Season it with pepper and salt to taste.
7. Spread the carn "bread" on the insides of the turkey, coating it well.

8. Place the duck, skin side down, on top of the "bread" stuffing, then spread the ground beef on the inside of the duck, coating it well.
9. Finally, place the chicken skin-side down on the beef and stuff it with the shrimp stuffing.
10. You can save any leftover stuffings for later.
11. When you are finished layering the birds, take the sides of the turkey and fold them together. Use stainless steel sealer clips or another person's help to hold the turkey closed, then begin to sew the bird closed. The stitches should be around 1-1 1/2 inch apart.
12. When you're done stitching, tie the turkey's legs together above the hip bones.
13. Place the bird in a large roasting tray, breast side up, and cook for about 4 1/2 to 5 hours.
14. Make sure to check with a meat thermometer you will insert in the thickest part on the bundled birds. The birds are ready once the thermometer reaches 180F.

Nutritional Values (Per Serving):

Calories: 1,422
Fat: 58.1g
Saturated Fat: 23g
Trans Fat: 4g
Carbohydrates: 0g
Fiber: 0g
Sodium: 822mg
Protein: 206g

Ultimate Beef Burgers

Prep Time: 15 mins.

Cooking Time: 20 mins.

Number of Servings: 14

Ingredients:

3lbs beef chuck, ground

1lb beef brisket, ground

12oz beef short ribs, boneless and ground

Sea salt

Black pepper

1 tbsp ghee

Directions:

1. In a bowl, add all three of the ground meats and mix well until evenly combined
2. Form into burger patties, around 5oz each
3. Season both sides with salt and pepper to taste
4. Place a non-stick skillet over high heat and let it get very hot
5. Add the ghee, waiting for it to melt if hardened, then cook the burgers for about 5 minutes per side until they are charred. Cook longer if you want them more well done.
6. Serve immediately

Nutritional Values (Per Serving):

Calories: 195
Fat: 12.7g
Saturated Fat: 5.6g
Trans Fat: 0.2g
Carbohydrates: 0g
Fiber: 0g
Sodium: 65mg
Protein: 18.6g

Buttered Scallops

Prep Time: 20 mins.

Cooking Time: 5 mins.

Number of Servings: 12

Ingredients:

4 tablespoons butter

2lbs scallops, cleaned

Salt

Pepper

Directions:

1. In a skillet over medium heat, melt 4 tablespoons of the butter and heat.
2. Add half of the scallops into the skillet and season them with salt and pepper to taste.
3. Cook for 2 minutes or until they become golden, then flip and cook for another 2 minutes.
4. Remove from heat and set aside, then cook the second batch of scallops. This might not be needed depending on the size of your skillet.
5. Serve hot with extra pepper and salt.

Nutritional Values (Per Serving):

Calories: 152
Fat: 9g
Saturated Fat: 4.7g
Trans Fat: 0g
Carbohydrates: 0g
Fiber: 0g
Sodium: 133mg
Protein: 16g

Rabbit Roast

Prep Time: 10 mins.

Cooking Time: 90 minutes

Number of Servings: 4

Ingredients:

1 rabbit, cleaned and chopped into pieces around 3lbs

1 tablespoon black pepper

1 teaspoons salt

2 cups broth

¼ cup butter

Directions:

1. Preheat your oven to 350F
2. Season the rabbit with salt and pepper to taste.
3. In a large pan over medium-high heat, melt the butter.
4. Place the rabbit in the pan and cook until brown on all sides.
5. Transfer to a deep baking dish then pours the broth over the rabbit.
6. Bake for 90 minutes until very tender, frequently basting with melted butter

Nutritional Values (Per Serving):

Calories: 630
Fat: 33g
Saturated Fat: 8g
Trans Fat: 0.2g
Carbohydrates: 0g
Fiber: 0g
Sodium: 1684g
Protein: 64g

Pluck Kabobs

Prep Time: 20 mins.

Cooking Time: 10 mins.

Number of Servings: 6

Ingredients:

4lb veal pluck including sweetbreads, cleaned

Sea salt

Black pepper

Skewers

Directions:

1. Make sure the pluck is cleaned off any arteries and connective tissues. If you're not sure, ask your butcher
2. Chop pluck into half-inch pieces
3. Turn on your grill and bring it to medium-high heat
4. Begin threading the pluck on the skewers making sure to include some variations on each skewer
5. Season thoroughly with salt and pepper to ensure the livers won't stick to the grill
6. Grill until they're charred on all sides

Nutritional Values (Per Serving):

Calories: 450
Fat: 23g
Saturated Fat: 10g
Trans Fat: 1g
Carbohydrates: 0g
Fiber: 0g
Sodium: 245mg
Protein: 62g